MW01093533

SERMON IN A SENTENCE

St. Thérèse of Lisieux

SERMON IN A SENTENCE

*A Treasury of Quotations
on the Spiritual Life*

FROM THE WRITINGS OF

St. Thérèse of Lisieux

DOCTOR OF THE CHURCH

*Arranged According to the Virtues of
The Holy Rosary
and Other Spiritual Topics*

Selected and Arranged by
JOHN P. McCLERNON

IGNATIUS PRESS   SAN FRANCISCO

Cover art by Christopher J. Pelicano
Cover design by Roxanne Mei Lum

Frontispiece by Edith Beckwith Smith
Combermere, Ontario, Canada

© 2002 Ignatius Press, San Francisco
All rights reserved
ISBN 0–89870–884–2
Library of Congress Control Number 2001095545
Printed in the United States of America ∞

Let the children come to me,

do not hinder them;

for to such belongs the kingdom of God

—Mark 10:14

DEDICATION

This work is dedicated to my wonderful and supportive wife, Mary, and to the five beautiful children with whom the Lord has blessed us and given us to share our lives: Christopher, Clare, Catherine, David, and Stephen.

Special thanks to my mother, Judy McClernon, a secular Carmelite, whose prayers, advice, and insights were so helpful. She continues to show me the "little way", not only by her words, but even more powerfully by her life.

I also wish to thank St. Thérèse, the Little Flower, who inspired me "in little ways" to go on with this project. It is she who really is the author and writer of this "Sermon in a Sentence". I am honored and privileged to be just an instrument.

Contents

Other Topics

INTRODUCTION

Many Catholics would like nothing better than to read the actual writings of the Church's spiritual giants. Taking time apart from busy life-styles to spend a few minutes with a saint promises precisely the kind of nourishment their souls need in today's secular culture. Imagine spending a few minutes with St. Thérèse of Lisieux, now a Doctor of the Church and perhaps the best known and loved of all modern saints. Her simple, direct, and sure way to holiness has helped many gain a better understanding of the spiritual life and a deeper union with Christ. This book has been designed to bring the inspiration of her words to you in a format that is as simple and direct as her own "little way".

Hundreds of short quotations taken from the writings and sayings of St. Thérèse have been classified by the Christian virtues of which they speak and then arranged to complement the fifteen-decade rosary, proceeding from the first joyful mystery (the Annunciation, with its virtue of humility) to the fifth glorious mystery (the Crowning of Mary, with its virtue of devotion to Mary). For those who choose to use these excerpts for meditation while reciting the rosary, we have placed a type ornament after the tenth one, to mark the end of a decade. Additional quotations follow, for use with a rosary or for separate meditation. A small selection of quotations on other topics of interest follows, bringing the reader a sample of Thérèse's unique insights into such subjects as the Eucharist, the Church, the Bible, and other saints.

It is hoped that this little book will serve as an irresistible introduction to one of our world's greatest spiritual masters. May she guide you along the path she blazed, straight into heaven! And along the way, may you find yourself surrounded by many spiritual rose petals, a gift from God's "Little Flower" to you.

ACKNOWLEDGMENTS

The author gratefully acknowledges permissions granted to reprint from the following sources:

Complete Spiritual Doctrine of St. Therese of Lisieux, by Reverend François Jamart, O.C.D. Translated by Reverend Walter Van de Putte, C.S.S.P. New York: Alba House, 1961. © 1961, by the Society of St. Paul, New York, N.Y.

The Story of a Soul: The Autobiography of Saint Thérèse of Lisieux, edited by Mother Agnes of Jesus. Translated by Michael Day, Cong. Orat. Rockford, Ill.: TAN Books and Publishers, 1997. First published in 1951 by Burns and Oates, Ltd. ©1951, and 1997, Burns, Oates, and Washbourne, Ltd. The Continuum International Publishing Group. Reprinted with the permission of the Publisher.

The Voice of the Saints: Counsels from the Saints to bring comfort and guidance in daily living. Selected and arranged by Francis W. Johnston. Rockford, Ill.: TAN Books and Publishers, 1986. First published in 1965 by Burns and Oates, Ltd. London. ©1965, Burns, Oates, and Washbourne. The Continuum International Publishing Group. Reprinted with the permission of the Publisher.

Scripture quotations have been taken from the following editions of the Holy Bible:

Abbreviations

C   Francois Jamart, O.C.D. *Complete Spiritual Doctrine of St. Therese of Lisieux*. Translated by Walter Van de Putte. New York: Alba House, 1961.

S   Thérèse of Lisieux. *The Story of a Soul*. Edited by Mother Agnes of Jesus. Translated by Michael Day. Rockford, Ill.: TAN Books and Publishers, 1997.

V   *The Voice of the Saints*. Edited by Francis W. Johnston. Rockford, Ill.: TAN Books and Publishers, 1993.

St. Thérèse of Lisieux

(1873–1897)

Doctor of the Church

Patroness of the Missions—Patroness of France

During her nine years in a Carmelite convent, Thérèse Martin did not stand out among the devout nuns with whom she shared her life. She never went to the missions, nor did she ever found a religious order or accomplish any notable great works or heroic deeds. Yet her "little way" of spiritual perfection has inspired millions of Catholics, who have found in St. Thérèse's message a practical and simple way to embrace sanctity. The "Little Flower", as she is affectionately known around the world, paved a way of holiness we can all follow. Her way is, in her own words, "the way of spiritual childhood" and consists of sanctifying one's life by trusting with childlike confidence and abandonment in Jesus, while loving Him through perfect fidelity to one's duties in life. To St. Thérèse, it is recognizing God and serving Him in the small daily sacrifices, instead of great deeds, that is the short and sure way to holiness of life.

Thérèse was born in Alençon, France, in 1873, the youngest of five living children (all girls) to Louis and Zélie Martin. The Martin family provided a truly devout Catholic home for the young Thérèse, and it was her parents' and older sisters' understanding of the spiritual life, their love and example that gave Thérèse a keen grasp of Christian virtue even in her early years. She was her father's "little queen" and the family pet, very pretty, lively, and lovable.

Tragedy struck early for Thérèse, who lost her mother to breast cancer when she was only four years old. Louis Martin decided to move the family to Lisieux in order to be closer to relatives who lived there. The two oldest sisters, Marie and Pauline, took over the management of the Martin home and religious instruction of the family. Pauline eventually became like a second mother to the little Thérèse.

The Martins remained a very holy family, very close and united. However, the loss of her mother was a great blow to Thérèse, whose lively personality became more withdrawn and shy. She was in her own words quite oversensitive and touchy, quickly bursting into tears at the smallest slight or criticism she encountered. At eleven years of age, Thérèse would lose Pauline, her "second mother", not to disease or illness, but to the Carmelite convent in Lisieux. A few months later Thérèse became so ill with fever that it was thought she would die. While praying in front of a statue of the Blessed Mother, she saw Mary smile at her and was instantly cured. Later her oversensitivity would likewise be miraculously cured on Christmas Day 1886, this time by Jesus Himself. On that day Thérèse claimed that the Christ Child entered into her heart and gave her instant strength to overcome her feelings forever. She would refer to this healing as a spiritual conversion, and her life would not ever be the same.

As the years went on Thérèse would see two more sisters follow the Master's call to the religious life. Marie followed her sister Pauline by entering the Carmelite convent in Lisieux, while Léonie left home to become, first a Poor Clare nun and, then, a Visitation nun in Caen. This eventually left Thérèse alone with her father, Louis, and her sister Céline, who also planned to enter the convent. Year by year Thérèse felt an ever greater desire to live a consecrated religious life. At the age of fifteen she resolutely made up her mind to follow in the footsteps of her two older sisters and enter the Carmelite convent in Lisieux. Her father readily consented, but religious authorities refused to grant her permission. Thérèse would have to wait.

Her goal was quite lofty, as a girl of fifteen was considered too young for the austere and demanding Carmelite rule of life. When the convent prioress said No, Thérèse went to the bishop. When permission to enter was not granted by the bishop, she undauntedly decided to speak personally with Pope Leo XIII. Not long after this, Louis Martin took Thérèse and Céline on a pilgrimage to Rome, and while there, Thérèse took her lone chance and begged the Pope to allow her to enter. He simply said, "If the good God wills, you will enter." Her prayers and petitions were quickly answered, and Thérèse was given the necessary approval to enter the Carmelite monastery at the end of the year.

In April 1888, Thérèse joined Pauline and Marie in Carmel. True to form, Thérèse loved religious practices, liturgical prayer, and the reading of Scripture. The novice mistress at that time would later testify at Thérèse's beatification that "from her entrance she astonished the community by her bearing, which was marked by a certain majesty that one would not expect in a child of fifteen." She was certainly a daughter of the King of

Kings, and her uncompromising love for Jesus, and confidence in His fatherly love for her, knew no bounds. Thérèse did not just want to be good, her overwhelming passion was to be a saint. She was consumed by her love for Love itself. Her impatience would manifest itself only in her strides to sanctity.

Thérèse considered herself far too small and imperfect to climb the stairs of perfection practiced by earlier saints. "I will look for some means of going to heaven by a little way which is very short and very straight, a little way that is new." Holy Scripture would hold the key to her "little way". Thérèse was inspired by the passage where Jesus states, "Let the little ones come to me, for it is to such as these that the kingdom of God belongs." Her vocation was simply to love Jesus, as His child, through perfect fidelity to His will for her. The little way was the way of spiritual childhood. She later wrote, "Sanctity is an interior disposition which makes us humble and little in God's arms, conscious of our weakness and trusting even to audacity in the goodness of our Father." The little way was one of perfect obedience, prayer, and sacrifice. She quickly developed a thirst to suffer for the love of God. All pain would be promptly offered to Jesus, while keeping it hidden under a smile. Thérèse embraced every opportunity to sacrifice and serve, no matter how small it seemed.

In 1889 her father, Louis, after two paralytic strokes, suffered a mental breakdown and had to be removed to a private sanitarium. He would remain there for three years. This would be a grievous sorrow to Thérèse, whose great love and trust in God was initially formed by her love and trust in her father, Louis. At his death in 1894, Céline, who had been taking care of him, would also enter the Carmelite convent in Lisieux, the fourth Martin girl to do so.

In spite of poor health, Thérèse from the start carried out all the austerities of the Carmelite rule. She developed tuberculosis over time and began to cough up blood in 1896. Thérèse kept working and suffering this way without telling anyone until she became so sick a year later that all knew of it. The joy and confidence that marked her days were now gone. Tuberculosis made a steady advance on her health and strength. Despite extreme bodily and spiritual sufferings, Thérèse appeared smiling and cheerful to all. Her success at this was so great that some of her fellow nuns thought she was pretending to be sick.

We owe a great deal to Mother Agnes (her sister Pauline), who as prioress at the time ordered Thérèse in 1894 to write the story of her childhood. A few years later the next prioress requested her to continue writing about her life in the convent. These two works were later combined into what is now known as the *Story of a Soul*. This book, although intended to be a journal for the eyes of nuns, would become seemingly overnight one of the great modern classics of the spiritual life. Here is enshrined forever her "little way", a message that is still as simple, practical, and compelling today as it was over one hundred years ago. Pope Benedict XV would later state that "her little way contained the secret for sanctity for the entire world."

St. Thérèse would not live long after completing the story of her life. In her twenty-third year she fell seriously ill in her bout with tuberculosis, and the remainder of her life was the spiritual martyrdom that she had longed for. During her final illness she was often fatigued, racked with intense pain, and plunged into spiritual dryness. The final chapter in her book is a tribute to the divine love of God. She concludes: "I entreat Thee to let Thy divine eyes rest upon a vast number of little souls; I entreat Thee to choose in this world a legion of little victims of Thy love."

Thérèse would finish the last pages of her manuscript while sitting in a wheelchair, too weak even to use a pen. As death approached, she was asked for some word of farewell, to which she replied, "I have said all . . . all is consummated . . . only love counts." She died on September 30, 1897, with her final words "My God . . . I love Thee!"

The speed and magnitude at which *Story of a Soul* caught fire around the globe is nothing short of a religious phenomenon. Many miracles, conversions, and graces have been and continue to be attributed to the intercession of this great saint. Thérèse seemed instinctively to know this would occur even before she died. To quote her once again, "If my wishes are granted, my heaven will be spent on earth until the end of the world. I want to spend my heaven doing good on earth."

Pope Pius XI canonized Thérèse in 1925. Two years later she would be named patroness of the missions, along with St. Francis Xavier. In 1944 both she and St. Joan of Arc were named co-patronesses of France. Pope John Paul II recently declared Thérèse a Doctor of the Catholic Church.

THE
JOYFUL
MYSTERIES

The First Joyful Mystery

The Annunciation of Our Lord

Humility

Whoever humbles himself like this child, he is the greatest in the kingdom of heaven.—Matthew 18:4

Sanctity is an interior disposition which makes us humble and little in God's arms, conscious of our weakness and trusting even to audacity in the goodness of our Father. (C 16)

[Spiritual childhood] also means not to attribute to ourselves the virtues we practice, not to believe that we are capable of anything, but to acknowledge that it is the good Lord who has placed that treasure in the hand of His little child that He may use it when He needs it. (C 28)

Humility is truth. (C 35)

It is proper to divine love to lower itself; hence, the lower we are, the more we attract God. (C 35)

We would like never to fall. What an illusion! What does it matter, my Jesus, if I fall at every moment? I come to recognize by it how weak I am and that is gain for me. You see by that how little I am able to do and You will be more likely to carry me in Your arms. (C 39)

If I am humble, I am entitled, without offending the good Lord, to do small foolish things until I die. (C 39)

The practice of humility consists not only in thinking and saying that you are full of faults, but in rejoicing because others think and say the same thing about you. (C 42)

In order to enjoy the merciful love of Jesus, it is necessary to humiliate ourselves, to acknowledge our nothingness, and this is a thing which many are unwilling to do. (C 43)

God wants humility of heart. If we were stronger, we would not need His help. But when He sees that we are convinced of our nothingness ... and appeal to Him, He stoops towards us and gives with divine generosity. (C 44)

Let us consider ourselves little and in need of God's support at every instant. As soon as He sees that we are truly convinced of our nothingness, He extends His hand to us. (C 45)

Since humility is so important, it is evident that no one is excused from practicing it. It is necessary to all, irrespective of their dignity or age. (C 47)

I experience great joy not only when others recognize my imperfection but, above all, when I realize myself that I am imperfect. (C 56)

It is Jesus who does everything in me; I do nothing, except remain little and weak. (C 68–69)

Instead of making me vain, the recollection of God's gifts to me leads me to Him.... If it pleases Him to make me appear better than I am, that is not my concern. He is free to do what He likes. (C 146–47)

As soon as I am pitied and flooded with attentions, I no longer have joy. (C 214)

I never want to ask God for greater sufferings, for these, then, would be my sufferings. I would have to bear them alone and I have never succeeded in doing anything unaided. (C 220)

Our Lord needs from us neither great deeds nor profound thoughts. Neither intelligence nor talents. He cherishes simplicity. (V 108)

It was well that our Lord told us: "In My Father's house there are many mansions." If there are some for great souls, for the Fathers of the desert, and the martyrs of penance, there must also be one for little children. And in that one, a place is kept for us if we but love Him dearly. (V 109)

The only glory which matters is the glory which lasts forever . . . one does not have to perform shining deeds to win that, but to hide one's acts of virtue from others, and even oneself. (S 47)

Real nobility is in the soul, not in name. (S 84)

The one who chose for love of God to be the poorest and most obscure on earth will be the first and the richest and most glorious in Heaven. (S 85)

I concentrated most of all on hidden acts of virtue. (S 118)

My act of humility acted like a charm in putting the devil to flight. (S 121)

Enlightenment on my nothingness does me more good than enlightenment on matters of faith. (S 161)

Only God can see what is in the bottom of our hearts; we are half-blind. (S 164)

In practice one finds that one can no more do good to souls without God's help than make the sun shine in the night. (S 168)

Those who do not mind whether they get attention and respect or not, find themselves surrounded by every kind of love. (S 176)

What a very little soul I am! I can only offer very little things to God. These little sacrifices bring great peace of soul. (S 181)

I have only to glance at the Gospels; at once this fragrance from the life of Jesus reaches me, and I know which way to run: to the lowest, not the highest place.
(S 189–90)

In my "little way" everything is most ordinary; everything I do must be within the reach of other little souls also. (S 214)

I implore Thee, dear Jesus, to send me a humiliation whensoever I try to set myself above others. (V 54)

Let us humbly take our place among the imperfect.
(C 45)

I want to hide in this world; I want to be the last in all things, for You, my Jesus. (C 36)

To ravish Thee, quite little I shall remain;
My self forgetting, I'll charm Thy loving Heart. (C 36)

Have recourse to the good Lord, recognize your faults,
and humble yourself. (C 287)

He does not call those who are worthy but those He
chooses to call. (S 1)

If we are still trying to do something great, even under
the pretext of zeal, our good Lord Jesus leaves us alone.
(C 45)

The Second Joyful Mystery

The Visitation of Elizabeth

Love of Neighbor

You shall love your neighbor as yourself.
—Mark 12:31

They [your critics] are the losers; they lose interior joy, for there is nothing sweeter than to think well of one's neighbor. (C 56)

There is only one thing for us to do during the night of this life: to love, to love Jesus with all the strength of our heart, and to save souls for Him that He may be loved. Oh! the joy of causing Jesus to be loved! (C 164)

Suffering makes us good; it makes us indulgent towards others, because suffering brings us nearer to the good Lord. (C 169)

Oh! how happy I would be, if, at the moment of my death, I were able to offer one soul to Jesus! There would be one soul which had been saved from hell and which would praise God for all eternity! (C 171–72)

I felt a great desire to labor for the conversion of sinners. . . . I felt charity enter my heart, the need to forget myself that I might please others, and from that time I have been happy. (C 182)

How easily we become impatient. We ought to be charitable and indulgent towards all without exception. (C 189)

When we have to deal with a disagreeable character, let us not lose heart and let us never give [the person] up. (C 287–88)

We should never fear the battle when the good of our neighbor is involved. (C 289)

We must reprove others at the cost of our personal tranquility and we must do this much less in order to open the eyes of our subjects, than to serve God. He will take care of the results. (C 289)

We should not be justices of the peace but angels of peace. (C 289)

Be very kind ... it is both an act of charity and an exercise of patience. (C 97)

We must sweeten our minds by charitable thoughts. After that, the practice of patience will become almost natural. (C 97)

When our Lord withdrew into solitude, the people followed Him and He did not send them away. . . . Imitate Him by receiving [others] graciously. (C 99)

I lose nothing, what I do is done for God . . . to give pleasure to Our Good Lord . . . so I am always paid for the trouble I take in serving others. (C 95)

I must anticipate the desires of others . . . show that we are much obliged, very honored to be able to render service. The good Lord wants me to forget myself in order to give pleasure to others. (C 94)

Charity consists in disregarding the faults of our neighbor, not being astonished at the sight of their weakness, but in being edified by the smallest act of virtue we see them practice. (C 92)

Jesus loves a cheerful heart. He loves persons who are always smiling. (C 93)

We must never refuse anyone, even when it costs us much pain. Think that it is Jesus who is asking this service of you; how eager and friendly you will then be in granting the favor requested. (C 93)

It is only the first step that is difficult. God will help us when we have good will. Just the desire alone of practicing charity gives peace to the soul. (C 100)

Fraternal charity is everything on this earth. We love God in the measure in which we practice charity. (C 101)

I don't know how to save up. All that I have I immediately spend for the purchase of souls. All that belongs to me belongs to everyone. (C 103)

Let us then work together for the salvation of souls. We have only this short life to save them and thus to give to the Lord the proof of our love. (C 105)

Lift up your eyes and see: see how in heaven there are empty places. It is your task to fill them. (C 104)

I feel that Jesus asks of us . . . to quench His thirst, by giving Him souls. . . . He begs souls from us. (C 106–7)

Charity took possession of my heart, making me forget myself, and I have been happy ever since. (S 66)

All we accomplish, however brilliant, is worth nothing without love. (S 130)

I too am judged by the Lord; I am judged by Jesus. I will never think uncharitably of anyone so that He may judge me leniently, or rather, not at all. (S 154)

A love which does not prove itself in action is not enough, nor is our natural readiness to please a friend; that is not charity, for sinners are ready to do the same. (S 155)

It is so much more generous to give than merely to lend. (S 158)

Often a single word, a friendly smile, is enough to give a depressed or lonely soul fresh life. (S 177)

Once a soul has been captivated by the odor of Your ointments, she cannot run alone . . . she draws all the souls she loves after her. (S 185)

Pray for the sick who are at the hour of death! Oh how much we should pray for the dying! (C 189)

I prefer to be sent away from the monastery . . . than to be wanting in my duty and failing to warn you for the good of your soul. (C 290)

If we want to live a life of love of God, we must not fail in our love towards our neighbor. (C 91)

In order to open that kingdom, He chose to die on a Cross, saying that there is no greater love than that of laying down one's life for those whom one loves. (C 100)

During the short moments that still remain to us on earth, let us not waste our time.... Let us save souls; let us be apostles. (C 106)

I tell Him I am quite happy that the eyes of my soul should be blind, while I am on earth, to the heavenly wonders in store for me, so long as He will open the eyes of unbelieving souls for all eternity. (S 146–47)

Charity must not remain hidden in the bottom of our hearts ... it must shine out not only to cheer those we love best, but ALL. (S 152)

I know that whenever I am charitable, it is Jesus alone who is acting through me and that the more closely I unite myself to Him, the more I will be able to love all. (S 153)

It is much harder to give to all who ask than to offer our services spontaneously; nor is it so hard to comply with a friendly request. (S 155)

Sentiments of charity are not enough; they must find expression. (S 159)

One must not despise anything that helps us to be more closely united to God. Such inspirations, however sublime, are worth nothing without deeds. (S 163)

One must completely forget one's own ideas and tastes, and guide souls along the particular path indicated for them by Jesus, not along one's own. (S 168)

Just as He gives the gardener the skill to tend rare and delicate plants while fertilizing them Himself, so He wishes to use others in His cultivation of souls. (S 79)

THE THIRD JOYFUL MYSTERY

THE BIRTH OF JESUS

Spirit of Poverty

Blessed are the poor in spirit, for theirs is the kingdom of heaven.—Matthew 5:3

[My way] is the way of spiritual childhood. (C 27)

My peace consists in remaining small. (C 42)

The thing that pleases Jesus when He beholds my soul is that I love my littleness and my poverty and have a blind hope in His mercy. (C 44)

The God of strength loves to show His power by making use of nothing. (C 44)

It is possible to remain little even when we are charged with the most formidable functions and . . . even when we are in extreme old age. (C 47)

Remain always little and poor, in order to expect everything from God. (C 49)

In order to love Jesus and be His victim of love, the weaker we are and the more completely without desires or virtues, the more we shall be disposed to receive the benefits of His consuming and transforming love working within us. (C 50)

Let us then remain far away from all that is vainglorious. Let us love our littleness, our lack of sensitivity. We shall then be poor in spirit and Jesus will come for us . . . and will set us afire with His love. (C 51)

I am very poor. It is the good Lord who provides me from moment to moment with the amount of help I need to practice virtue. (C 54)

Don't hoard anything. Give away your spiritual goods as quickly as you earn them. (C 55)

Our sole good consists in loving God with all our heart and being poor in spirit while we are in this world, . . . there is no joy like that of being truly poor in spirit. (C 57)

I merely extend my hand to You, like a small beggar child, and I am sure that You will fully satisfy me. (C 68)

Jesus became poor that we might practice charity towards Him. He longs for our love and begs for it. . . . He looks for souls who will console Him but finds none. . . . He, as it were, puts Himself at our mercy. (C 170)

Jesus alone IS; all the rest IS NOT. (C 262)

I know that Jesus is in me. . . . He it is who does everything in me; I do nothing. (C 262)

God is a Father. Allow Him to act as He pleases. He knows well what His very small baby needs. (C 285)

The Lord is often pleased to give wisdom to little ones. (C 286)

In order to love You as You love me, I must borrow Your own love. (C 77)

The greatest honor God can do a soul is not to give it much, but to ask much of it. (V 115)

In the world of souls, the living garden of the Lord, it pleases Him to create great Saints, who may be compared with the lilies or the rose; but He has also created little ones, who must be content to be daisies or violets. (S 2)

Our Lord's love shines out just as much through a little soul who yields completely to His grace as it does through the greatest. (S 3)

He has, in fact, created the child, who knows nothing and can only make feeble cries. . . . It is to hearts such as these that He stoops. What delights Him is the simplicity of these flowers of the field. (S 3)

Leave the riches that will fade for those of Heaven.
(S 49)

God has given me the grace not to be disheartened by any transitory things. (S 63)

Joy does not reside in the things about us, but in the very depths of the soul. . . . One can have it in the gloom of a dungeon as well as in the palace of a king. (S 99)

Poverty consists in lacking not only little luxuries, but even things one could not do without. In the dark, I found my soul flooded with divine light. (S 117)

What peace floods a soul when it soars above natural feelings! The joy of the truly poor in spirit is beyond all compare. (S 156)

Love alone can make us pleasing to God, so I desire no other treasure. (S 192)

In order to belong to Jesus we must be little, but there are few souls who aspire to remain in that littleness. (C 43)

To consent to remain always poor and powerless, there lies the difficulty! ... Where can we find one who is truly poor? Is not he alone truly poor who is so humble-minded that he believes himself to be nothing? (C 51)

It is my weakness that gives me the audacity of offering myself as a victim of His love. (C 154)

The secrets of perfection [are] secrets hidden from their vast science, a knowledge which requires poverty of spirit. (C 231)

It was Jesus, the Director of directors, who instructed me in the science which is hidden from scholars and the wise, but which He deigns to reveal to little ones. (C 247)

You alone, O Jesus, could fill my soul;
For boundless was the need I felt of loving You. (C 262)

We must love our nothingness in His Infinite All, and think only of this All which is infinitely lovable. (C 263)

Our mission is to forget ourselves, to annihilate ourselves. We are so insignificant and, yet, Jesus wants the salvation of souls to depend on our sacrifices, on our love. (C 106–7)

THE FOURTH JOYFUL MYSTERY

THE PRESENTATION IN THE TEMPLE

Obedience

If you love me, you will keep my commandments.
—John 14:15

In Heaven, the good Lord will do all that I want, because on earth I never did my own will. (C 21)

My only aim would be to accomplish the will of the good Lord, to sacrifice myself for Him in a manner that would please Him. (C 205)

All is grace.... We should adore God's will whatever it may be. (C 208)

To say we suffer in peace does not mean that we suffer with joy, at least with a joy that is felt. In order to suffer in peace, it is enough to will truly all that Jesus wills. (C 218)

The way I am following brings me no consolation and yet it gives me all consolations, for it is Jesus who has chosen it and all I want is to please Him alone, yes, Him alone! (C 234)

If we wish to be holy, we have merely to unite ourselves to Jesus, endeavoring to please Him. (C 263)

Serve God. He will take care of the results. (C 289)

I have no difficulty in bearing the burden of obedience. (C 84)

Even if all were to fail in the observance of the rule, that would not be a reason for justifying ourselves. (C 84)

We do not bargain when we love. Jesus teaches me not to refuse Him anything and to be pleased when He gives me an opportunity for proving to Him that I love Him. I do this peacefully, with complete abandonment. (C 82)

Perfection consists in doing the will of God, in being what He wants us to be. (C 83)

I did my best to please Jesus in all my actions and was very careful never to offend Him. (C 76)

If you wish to be a saint, it is very easy . . . aim only at pleasing Jesus, at uniting yourself intimately with Him. (C 75)

To have beautiful and holy thoughts and to write books on lives of the saints do not count as much as answering as soon as you are called. (S xiv)

Jesus made me realize that simple obedience would please Him best. (S 1)

I am not afraid to suffer for Your sake; I only fear doing my own will, so I give it to You and choose everything You will. (S 13)

I came to love God more and more as I grew up and often offered my heart to Him. . . . I used to try hard to please Jesus in everything I did and never offend Him.
(S 22)

I wanted above all else to serve Him and give Him glory.
(S 77)

In the depths of my soul I never ceased to have the profoundest peace because I sought the will of God alone. (S 83)

If I really belonged to Jesus as His plaything, to console and entertain Him, it was for me to do what He wanted, not what I wanted. (S 116)

I offer myself to You, my Beloved, that You may do in me everything You will. (S 121–22)

I set myself, as never before, to do everything to please my Heavenly Spouse, the King of Kings. (S 123)

Now I am guided by self-abandonment alone and need no other compass; no longer knowing how to ask for anything with eagerness except that God may do His will completely in my soul. (S 133)

All is well when one seeks nothing but the Divine Will.
(S 140)

I try to do everything to give pleasure to Our Lord.
(S 177)

My heart is filled to the brim with the Will of Our Lord, so that nothing else can find place there, but glides across like oil over tranquil waters. (S 211)

I will only what He wills, and it is what He does that pleases me. I do not fear the last struggle nor any pain involved in my illness, however severe. (S 212)

Thy will be done, my God, but have mercy on me; sweet Virgin Mary, aid me. (S 215)

The happier they are to be as He wills, the more perfect they are. (S 2)

One could be a Saint in varying degrees, for we are free to respond to Our Lord's invitation by doing much or little in our love for Him; to choose, that is, among the sacrifices He asks. (S 13)

THE FIFTH JOYFUL MYSTERY

THE FINDING OF THE CHILD JESUS
IN THE TEMPLE

Piety

You . . . must be perfect as your heavenly Father is perfect.
—Matthew 5:48

The Way of Spiritual Childhood . . . is the only means to make rapid progress in love and the only way by which saints are made. (C 47)

Our Lord has one great weakness. He is blind and He really knows nothing about arithmetic. He does not know how to add, but to blind Him and prevent Him from adding the smallest sum . . . you must take Him by His Heart. This is his weak spot. (C 66)

Take Jesus by His Heart. . . . It is this way that I took hold of the good Lord and that is why I shall be well received by Him. (C 66)

Practice all the virtues and so always lift up your little foot to mount the ladder of holiness. (C 69)

The good Lord does not demand more from you than good will.... He looks at you with love. Very soon, won over by your useless efforts, He will come down and take you in His arms. He will carry you up. (C 69)

I know that there are saints who spent their lives practicing extraordinary mortifications ... but, after all, there are many mansions in the house of our heavenly Father. Jesus has told us so and that is why I follow the way He has traced out for me. (C 142)

The best rule is that we should follow what love inspires us to do from moment to moment, with the sole desire of pleasing the good Lord in everything He asks of us. (C 143)

More love is required of those who have received more. Hence, I do my best to make my life one act of love. (C 146)

Live in one great act of perfect love. (C 152)

Words are not enough. In order to be truly a victim of love, we must give ourselves entirely. We shall be consumed by love to the extent that we surrender ourselves to love. (C 155)

Our intention ... is that we may make our lives one great act of perfect love, that we may love God with His own love; that we may strive for a holiness that will cause Love to be loved by others. (C 158)

I have said all. All is fulfilled. It is only love that matters.
(C 165)

It is necessary to suffer much if we want to attain holiness.
(C 172)

[And what do you say to Jesus?] I say nothing to Him; I just love Him. (C 190)

We should get hold of Jesus through His heart and smother Him with caresses. (C 262)

When I am as it were without feeling, seem unable to pray or practice virtue, that is the time when I must look around for little opportunities, for "nothings" which please Jesus . . . , for example a smile, a kind word. (C 233)

We have only one task during the night of the present life . . . to love Jesus. (C 262)

To love means giving everything and giving ourselves. I love Him so much that I am always satisfied with anything He sends me. I love all that He does. (C 83)

Merit does not consist in doing or giving much. It consists of loving much. (C 75)

People advance in perfection by performing a great number of acts of virtue, and they are right. But my Director, who is Jesus Himself, teaches me to do everything through love. (C 75)

It is only through love that we can render ourselves pleasing to the good Lord, that love is the one thing I long for. The science of love is the only science I desire. (C 74)

I know of no other means to reach perfection than by love. To love; how perfectly our hearts are made for this!

(C 74)

You ask me for a method of attaining perfection. I know of love—and only love. Love can do all things. (V 21)

You cannot be half a Saint. You must be a whole Saint or no Saint at all. (V 147)

To become a Saint, one has to suffer much, always aim at perfection and forget oneself. (S 13)

God often asks no more than the desire to work for His glory. (S 148)

I am far from doing what I know I ought to do, but the very desire to do so brings me peace. (S 158)

If only everyone weak and imperfect like me felt as I do, no one would despair of reaching the heights of love, for Jesus does not ask for glorious deeds. He asks only for self-surrender and for gratitude. (S 193)

He does not need our works, only our LOVE. (S 193)

Charity gave me the key to my vocation. . . . All vocations are summed up in love and that love is all in all, embracing every time and place because it is eternal. (S 199)

I feel that my mission is just beginning, my mission of making others love the good Lord as I love Him and giving to souls my "Little Way". (C 9)

It is only the complete immolation of self that can be called love, and it is by means of suffering that we sanctify ourselves. (C 172)

I would beg the good Lord to accomplish in me . . . to sanctify me as much in a few years, as I might have been sanctified had I reached a ripe old age, so that I might be quickly consumed in love. (C 209)

To be with You, and in You, this is my one and only desire. (C 262)

When Jesus looks at a soul, He immediately gives to it a divine resemblance; but it is necessary that it constantly keep its eyes focused on Him alone. (C 263)

I find it very easy to practice perfection, for I realize that we have merely to take Jesus by His Heart. (C 74)

We cannot all be alike; there must be different kinds of holiness to glorify the divine perfections. (C 135)

How easily one might become so taken up with one-self that one might forget the glorious purpose of one's vocation. (S 88)

THE
SORROWFUL
MYSTERIES

The First Sorrowful Mystery

The Agony of Jesus in the Garden

Sorrow for Sin

The cares of the world, and the delight in riches, and the desire for other things, enter in and choke the word, and it proves unfruitful.—Mark 4:19

We must not be discouraged by our faults, for children fall frequently. (C 28)

I know the means for being always happy and drawing profit from my miseries. Jesus seems to encourage me on this road.... He teaches me to profit from everything, both from the good and the evil that I find in myself. (C 38)

I have many weaknesses but I am never astonished because of them. I am not always as prompt as I should like to be in rising above the insignificant things of this world. (C 39)

It is a great trial to see only the dark side of things.... Do what you can to detach your heart from earthly cares ... then feel certain that Jesus will do the rest. (C 40)

When we commit a fault, we should not blame it on a physical cause, such as illness or the weather, but attribute it to our own imperfection. (C 40)

When we accept with mildness the humiliation of having manifested our imperfection, the grace of God returns immediately. (C 41)

It is only when His children ignore their constant lapses and make a habit of them and fail to ask His pardon that Christ grieves over them. (C 41)

He is full of joy at the sight of those who love Him and, after each fault, ask His pardon and cast themselves in His arms. He then recalls only their desires of perfection. (C 41)

When we see that we are wretched, we no longer wish to look at ourselves but we gaze at our Beloved. We have merely to love Him, without looking at ourselves, without examining our faults too much. (C 45)

The weaker we are and the more we are without desires or virtues, the more are we receptive of the operations of God's love in us. (C 52)

Even if I had on my conscience all the sins that can be committed, I would go and cast myself in the arms of

Jesus with a heart torn by repentance, for I know how much He cherishes the prodigal child that returns to Him. (C 64)

The sorrow which casts us down is the hurt to our self-love. . . . To brood gloomily over our own imperfections paralyzes our soul. (C 64)

The memory of my faults humbles me; it causes me never to rely on my own strength, which is but weakness, but especially it teaches me a further lesson of the mercy and love of God. (C 65)

A glance of love towards Jesus and the knowledge of our profound misery makes reparation for everything.

(C 65)

We have only to beg pardon and all is repaired by that act of love. Jesus opens His Heart to us. He forgets our infidelities and does not want to recall them. He will do even more: He will love us even better than before we committed that fault. (C 65)

I entrust my infidelities to Jesus. . . . I believe that I shall in this way gain greater power over His Heart and attract more fully the love of Him who came not to call the just but the sinners. (C 66)

How easy it is to please Jesus. We have merely to love Him without paying attention to ourselves, without examining too intently our defects. With one glance towards Jesus comes the realization of our own wretchedness, and everything is in order once again. (C 147)

Love, which can draw profit from everything, soon consumes everything that might displease Jesus. He will even make our faults serve our progress, and all that will be left will be a humble and profound peace abiding in the depths of our hearts. (C 155)

Self-love soon comes along like an evil wind that extinguishes everything. (C 81)

If the greatest sinner on earth should repent at the moment of death, and draw his last breath in an act of love; neither the many graces he had abused, nor the many sins he had committed would stand in his way. Our Lord would receive him into His mercy. (V 24)

He wants me to love Him because He has forgiven me, not much, but everything. (S 57)

I soon found that the more one advances, the further off one sees the goal to be. (S 116)

Our Lord is more tender than any mother. . . . A mother is always ready to forgive her child's little involuntary faults. (S 125)

It is love rather than fear which leads us to avoid the smallest voluntary fault. (s 135)

Our Lord is just. He makes allowances for all our short-comings and knows full well how weak we are. What have I to fear then? (s 135–36)

Surely the God of infinite justice, who pardons the Prodigal Son with such mercy, will be just with me. (s 136)

I am sure that self-seeking leads to no good. (s 169)

Our Lord poured in the light of truth, which shines far brighter than the shadowy light of earthly pleasures.
(s 180)

I would not exchange ten minutes spent upon my act of charity for a thousand years of such worldly delights.
(s 180)

No one can make me frightened any more, because I know what to believe about His mercy and His love; I know that, in the twinkling of an eye, all those thousands of sins would be consumed as a drop of water cast into a blazing fire. (s 190)

I only ask one grace—may I never offend You. (s 145)

I must put up with myself as I am; full of imperfections, but I will find a little way to Heaven, very short and direct. (s 140)

The fact that people recognize your imperfection, well, that is as it should be; it is your gain. (C 56)

When I fall ... like a child, it makes me realize my nothingness and my weakness all the better and I say to myself: "What would become of me? What would I be able to accomplish if I were to rely on my own powers alone?" (C 40)

The Second Sorrowful Mystery

The Scourging at the Pillar

Purity

Clean the inside of cup and dish first so that the outside may become clean as well.—Matthew 23:26

Jesus is pleased to teach [me] the science of glorying in [my] infirmities. That is a great grace and I pray Jesus to teach it also to you, for there alone are found peace and repose of heart. (C 42)

Why should we defend ourselves when we are misunderstood and misjudged? Let us leave that aside. Let us not say anything.... O blessed silence, which gives so much peace to the soul. (C 46)

I prefer to be accused unjustly ... and joyfully offer this to the good Lord. Then I humble myself at the thought that I am indeed capable of doing the thing of which I have been accused. (C 46)

In the hidden struggle of interior renunciation, nature cannot get such a hold on us and we can more easily attain humility and peace. (C 142)

When something was wanting I was much more satisfied, because I was then truly giving up something.
(C 143)

It suffices that we refrain from indulging in a selfish sort
of happiness, and offer to our Spouse the small joys He
strews on the path of our life to delight our souls and
raise them even to Himself. (C 145)

Love is fed by and develops from sacrifice. The more
we deprive ourselves of natural satisfaction, the stronger
and the more disinterested our love [for others] becomes.
(C 146)

Our suffering never makes Him happy. He sends it to
us and, as it were, turns away His head while so doing,
but suffering is a thing that is necessary for us. (C 168)

Suffering is necessary to detach us from the earth and
make us look up higher than this world . . . to detach us
from all that is created . . . from all that is not Jesus, and
to purify us. (C 169)

O Jesus, Who art sweetness unspeakable, turn into bitterness to me all fleshly delights. (C 176)

The more intimate the suffering, the less it appears to
the eyes of others, the more it gladdens You (oh my
God). (C 214)

It is my belief that what Jesus did during that retreat was to try to detach me from everything that is not Himself ... If only you knew how great is my joy because I can please Jesus by having none.... This is a most subtle sort of joy and one that is not felt in any way. (C 232)

He wants everything for Himself alone. Well! I will give Him everything, everything! Even when I feel I have nothing to offer, I will give Him that nothing. (C 232)

Our love for Jesus is truly great when we do not feel its sweetness. It then becomes a martyrdom. (C 81)

When ... we begin to seek ourselves, true love dies away. (C 81)

I will give myself entirely to Him, for I want to live for Him alone. (C 78)

In the crucible of trials from within and without, my soul has been refined. (S 3)

My dresses, lovely as they were, and my presents— these could never fill my heart. Jesus alone could do that. (S 53)

It is so easy to miss your way when the paths of the world seem so attractive.... Enlightened souls find the pleasure which the world offers mixed with bitterness, while the immense void of their desires cannot be filled by a moment's flattery. (S 60)

I wanted so much to love Jesus with my whole heart and prove it in a thousand ways while I still had the chance. (S 69)

The simple and upright see no evil because it does not exist in inanimate things, only in impure hearts. (S 86)

My mortification consisted in checking my self-will; keeping back an impatient word, doing little things for those around me without their knowing and countless things like that. (S 103)

The Spouse of Virgins . . . loves His lilies to be white as snow. (S 113)

Jesus, my Divine Spouse, grant that I may ever keep my baptismal robe spotless. (S 121)

Moment by moment, the Merciful Love of God renews and cleanses me and leaves my heart without a trace of sin. (S 137)

A heart given to God loses none of its natural tenderness; on the contrary, the more pure and divine it becomes, the more such tenderness increases. (S 149)

The Third Sorrowful Mystery

The Crowning with Thorns

Courage

Courage! It is I! Do not be afraid.
—Matthew 14:27

I am not going to worry, but I will always stretch out my suppliant arms towards You with great love. I cannot believe that You would abandon me. (C 39)

Never be discouraged. (C 65)

Let us struggle without respite. Let us go on, however much we are tired of the struggle. Where would our merit be if we fought only when we feel courageous? (C 69)

It does not matter that you have no courage, provided you act as if you had courage. (C 69)

If you offered yourself to Divine Justice you might entertain fear, but merciful Love will have compassion on your weakness. . . . From this love we should expect nothing but mercy. (C 157)

It is suffering which makes us resemble Him. A spouse of Jesus must resemble Jesus. And He is covered with blood and crowned with thorns. (C 169)

I am not at all afraid of the last struggles nor of the suffering of illness, however serious they may be. The good Lord has helped me and led me by the hand from my most tender years. I count on Him. I feel certain that He will continue to assist me until the end. (C 187)

When you are ill . . . abandon yourself to the good Lord without any anxiety. . . . If He permits you to be wanting in anything, this is a grace. It means He trusts that you are sufficiently strong to suffer something for Him. (C 193)

We shall suffer together, as the early Christians suffered, keeping close together in order to encourage one another during our periods of trial. (C 197)

When I suffer much, when painful, disagreeable things happen to me, instead of looking sad, I try to smile. . . . It has now become a habit. (C 217)

Jesus prepares for us a chalice having the degree of bitterness which our feeble nature is able to bear. . . . He never asks of us a sacrifice that is beyond our strength. (C 219)

Doubt was impossible. Faith and hope were no longer necessary. Love revealed to us on earth the One whom our hearts were seeking. We had found Him and He had kissed us and no one in the future could despise us. (C 230)

If all souls that are weak and imperfect could feel what Your little Thérèse, the most insignificant of souls, feels, not one would despair of reaching the top of the mountain of Love. (C 245)

I have fought much; I am very tired but I am not afraid of battle. I am as much at peace there as during mental prayer. It is God's will that I should fight to the finish. (C 286)

I am not a warrior who has fought with earthly weapons, but I have fought with the sword of the spirit which is the word of God. . . . I shall die bearing arms. (C 291)

Smiling I brave the fire; and in Your arms, O my divine Bridegroom, with a song on my lips, I shall die on the field of battle, my weapons in my hand. (C 291)

What great grace is ours when, in the morning, we seem to be filled with lassitude and to lack both courage and strength to practice virtue! Then is the ideal moment to put the axe to the root of the tree. (C 82)

Discouragement itself is a form of pride. I wish, therefore, O my God, to build all my trust on You. (V 54)

Life is only a dream: soon we shall awaken. And what joy! The greater our sufferings, the more limitless our glory. Do not let us waste the trials Jesus sends. (V 125)

Unite [yourself] forever to His Divine Strength. (S 52)

By becoming little and weak for love of me, He made me strong and full of courage, and with the arms He gave me, I went from one victory to another, and began to "run as [a] giant". (S 64)

The divine call was always so urgent that, even if it had meant going through fire, I would have cast myself in to follow Him. (S 72)

Love of Jesus, and that alone, gave me the strength to face these difficulties. (S 80)

My path is certainly not one of fear. Our Lord Himself encourages me to follow it, and I always know how to be happy and profit from my miseries. (S 129)

Whenever I find myself faced with the prospect of an attack by my enemy, I am most courageous; I turn my back on him, without so much as looking at him, and run to Jesus. (S 146)

God is certainly very good to have lifted up my soul and lent it wings. The nets of the hunters can no longer frighten me. (S 161)

I want to do my duty, no matter what the cost, and Our Lord has given me the grace to face everything. (S 170)

You must not wish to see the fruit of your efforts. Jesus takes pleasure in keeping for Himself alone those nothings which console Him. (C 56)

The good Lord will not abandon me. . . . Yes, my God, everything You wish, but have pity on me. (C 191)

A soul in the state of grace need never be afraid of the devil, who is such a coward that even the gaze of a child will frighten him away. (S 14)

I am glad to fight side by side with them [Carmelite sisters] for the glory of the King of Heaven; but at the same time, I should be quite ready to go and fight on another battlefield, should the Divine General so wish. (S 149)

THE FOURTH SORROWFUL MYSTERY

THE CARRYING OF THE CROSS

Patience

[A]s for the [seeds] in the good soil, they are those who, hearing the word, hold it fast in an honest and good heart, and bring forth fruit with patience.—Luke 8:15

The glory of my Jesus, that is all. For my honor, I abandon it to Him, and if He seems to forget me, well! He is free to do so, for I no longer belong to myself but to Him. (C 37)

He will tire more quickly of making me wait than I shall tire of waiting for Him. (C 37)

To humble ourselves, to suffer our imperfections with patience, this is true sanctity, the source of peace. (C 47)

God's mercy exercises endless patience. (C 63–64)

I am willing to wait until the day which has no setting sun, and when my darksome faith will vanish at His sight.

(C 281)

When we engage ourselves in the way of love and offer ourselves as victims ... we are invited to surrender ourselves without reserve to God's good pleasure ... even to the extent of sharing with Jesus His cup of bitterness.

(C 157)

In one instant Jesus accomplished what I had been unable to do for several years, having been content, on my part, with my good will, which had never been wanting.

(C 182)

Just like the Apostles, I was able to say, Lord, I have fished all night and taken nothing. . . . Jesus Himself took hold of the net, cast it out and drew it in filled with fishes. He made me a fisher of souls. (C 182)

I felt an increase of strength after suffering each humiliation. (C 199)

Jesus suffered with sadness. Could we say that a soul was suffering if it did not experience sadness? And could we then claim that we are suffering generously, nobly ... what an illusion that would be! (C 216)

Why fear that you might not be able to carry that cross without growing weak? Didn't Jesus fall three times on His way to Calvary and you, poor little child, should you not resemble your Bridegroom? (C 216)

Would you want to refuse to fall a hundred times, if that were necessary to prove your love to Him, and to rise each time with renewed strength? (C 216)

We can bear much suffering, when we suffer it from moment to moment. (C 219)

Jesus gives me at every moment what I am able to bear and nothing more, and if the next moment He increases my suffering He also increases my strength. (C 220)

The King of Kings humbled Himself to such a degree that His Face was hidden and He could no longer be recognized. I too desire to hide my face ... that He alone should be able to number my tears, so that He may rest His head at least in my heart and feel that in it He is known and understood. (C 267)

The poor little bride of Jesus ... desires to gaze at the face of her Beloved merely that she may collect the tears that are flowing from those eyes that have ravished her by their hidden charms. (C 267)

Be another Veronica who wipes away the blood and tears of Jesus, her only Beloved. (C 268)

We must serve our Lord; sow what is good around us without worrying about its growth. For us the labors; for Jesus, success! (C 289)

We may be tempted to give up everything. However, we can repair everything and even gain in grace through an act of love, though it be unaccompanied by any sensible feeling. Jesus smiles. (C 83)

The tears He sheds over the wicked are wiped away by our poor, feeble efforts, by our small gift of love. (C 83)

When we shall see Him in Heaven, then we shall understand the price of suffering and trial. Like Jesus, we shall say: "It was truly necessary for suffering to try us and bring us to glory." (V 127)

I really ... had to go through many a storm before I reached the harbor of peace or tasted the fruits of total surrender and perfect love. (S 38)

Jesus bears that [our imperfections] patiently; He does not like teaching us everything at once, but normally enlightens us a little at a time. (S 116)

Every moment He is guiding and inspiring me. ... Most often it is not at prayer that they come, but while I go about my daily duties. (S 135)

I am perfectly content to go on suffering in body and soul for years, if that would please God. I am not in the least afraid of living for a long time; I am ready to go on fighting. (S 148)

God . . . never tires of waiting for some people, enlightening them only little by little, so I was careful not to rush things. (S 165)

If I did not suffer simply from moment to moment, I would find it impossible to be patient, but I look only at the present, forget the past and am careful never to anticipate the future. (S 211)

When we surrender to discouragement or despair, it is usually because we are thinking too much of the past or the future. (S 211)

Suffering may reach extreme limits but I am sure that the good Lord will never abandon me. (C 220)

THE FIFTH SORROWFUL MYSTERY

THE CRUCIFIXION

Self-Denial

If any man would come after me, let him deny himself and take up his cross daily and follow me.—Luke 9:23

There is only one thing for us to do here below: to throw at Jesus' feet the flowers of little sacrifices, to win Him through our caresses. That is the way in which I have taken hold of Him. (C 28)

Seek only to gather flowers, the flowers of sacrifice, and offer them to the good Lord for His pleasure. (C 28)

I have practiced self-forgetfulness. I have tried not to seek myself in anything. (C 47)

Offer Him the sacrifice of seeing all the flowers of your desires and good will fall to the ground without producing anything. In the twinkling of an eye, at the moment of your death, He will know how to bring forth rich, ripe fruit on the tree of your life. (C 56)

We must do all that lies in our power ... ; we must give without counting the cost; we must constantly renounce ourselves. In one word, we must prove our love by all the good works we can perform. (C 69)

If we can say that our sacrifices are like locks of hair that captivate the heart of Christ, we must likewise say that our joys affect Him in a like manner. (C 145)

Let us, therefore, make our life a continual sacrifice, a martyrdom of love to console Jesus. He asks only a glance, a sigh, but a glance and a sigh that are for Him alone. (C 170)

It is only suffering that can beget souls for Jesus. (C 171)

Jesus has for us a love so incomprehensible, so delicate, that He does not want to do anything without associating us with Him. He wants us to participate with Him in the work of saving souls. (C 171)

The Creator of the universe waits for prayers, for the immolation made by a poor insignificant soul, to save other souls which, like that soul, were bought at the price of all His blood. (C 171)

The cross has followed me from the cradle, but Jesus has taught me to love it passionately. (C 172)

Why worry about exterior crosses! The true cross is the martyrdom of the heart, the intimate suffering of the soul. (C 185)

I myself . . . draw great strength from renunciation. (C 204)

Our Lord died in anguish on the Cross and yet, He had the most beautiful death of love that ever was. (C 210)

I know one spring and having drunk from it you are still thirsty, but it is not a panting, gasping sort of thirst; on the contrary, it is very sweet, for it is satiating. This spring is suffering, a suffering known to Jesus alone. (C 214)

Jesus is there on His Cross. Since you have the privilege of receiving His love, He also wants to make you resemble Him. (C 216)

At the moment when He expired, Jesus gave to His Father the greatest proof of love that was possible. (C 252)

Jesus is thirsting more than ever for love. (C 76)

I am a little soul and I labor solely for His pleasure. I would be happy to suffer the greatest pains, were it only to make Him smile even once. (C 75)

Miss no single opportunity of making some small sacrifice, here by a smiling look, there by a kindly word; always doing the smallest things right, and doing it all for love. (V 79)

Believe me, the writing of pious books, the composing of the sublimest poetry; all that does not equal the smallest act of self-denial. (V 80)

You will have no difficulty in loving the Cross if you think often of the words: "He loved me and delivered Himself up for me." (V 123)

So every day, I made many sacrifices and acts of love, which were transformed into flowers.... I wanted all the flowers on earth to cradle Jesus in my heart. (S 49)

I made up my mind ... to stay in spirit at the foot of the Cross, to gather up the dew of heavenly life and give it to others. (S 66)

The cry of Jesus as He died, "I thirst", echoed every moment in my soul; inflaming my heart with a burning love. I longed to satisfy His thirst for souls; I was consumed myself with this same thirst, and yearned to save them from the everlasting fires of Hell, no matter what the cost. (S 66)

The only mortification which came my way was the mortification of self-love, but it did me much more good than corporal penances would have done. (S 118)

I desire nothing at all now except to love until I die of love. (S 148)

He thirsted for love, and He is more thirsty than ever now. . . . He finds so few surrendering themselves without reserve to the tenderness of His infinite love. (S 193)

I can prove my love only by scattering flowers, that is to say, by never letting slip a single little sacrifice, a single glance, a single word; by making profit of the very smallest actions, by doing them all for love. (S 202)

You flew down to this land of exile, to suffer and die, that You might bear all souls away and plunge them deep into the bosom of the Blessed Trinity, the eternal home of Love. (S 205)

Look at His adorable Face. Look at His glazed and sunken eyes. Look at His wounds. Look Jesus in the Face. There, you will see how He loves us. (V 124)

O Jesus, it is peace I beg of You. Peace, and above all, boundless love. Jesus, let me die for You, a martyr; grant me martyrdom of soul or of body, or better still, grant me both! (S 121)

Hoping to quench His thirst, I poured out His Blood on souls and offered them to Him, refreshed with this dew of Calvary, exchanging love for love. (S 68)

It had been the sight of His Blood flowing from one of these very Wounds that had given me my thirst for souls.

(S 67)

One must suffer to gain Eternal Life. (V 116)

I suffer much ... but I feel that I can bear still greater trials. (C 205)

My least desires have been fulfilled; hence, the greatest of all, to die of love, will also be accomplished. (C 209)

Jesus is our Spouse of blood. He wants for Himself all the blood of our heart.... I cannot understand the infinite love that prompted Him to treat me in this manner. (C 215)

Jesus made me understand that it was through the Cross that He desired to give me souls and, thus, I felt more and more attracted to suffering in proportion to its increase. (C 184)

Do such things [penance] with great simplicity. (C 143)

I prefer to practice mortification in a manner that leaves my mind more free [for God]. (C 143)

In those extraordinary penances there easily creeps in that which is inspired by nature rather than virtue. (C 142)

THE
GLORIOUS
MYSTERIES

THE FIRST GLORIOUS MYSTERY

THE RESURRECTION OF JESUS FROM THE DEAD

Faith

Blessed are those who have not seen and yet believe.
—John 20:29

[My way] is the "Way of Spiritual Childhood", the way of confidence and total abandonment to God. (C 9)

God would not give me the desire of doing good on earth, if He did not intend to fulfill it. (C 21)

God's will shall be accomplished in spite of the jealousy of men. (C 22)

If you are nothing, do not forget that Jesus is ALL. Hence, lose your little nothingness in His infinite ALL and think only of that ALL, who alone is lovable. (C 45)

I have no works. . . . I have confidence that He will render to me according to His own works. (C 55)

He teaches [me] how to speculate in the bank of His love. . . . He transacts that business Himself, without telling [me] how He does it, for that is His affair. (C 56)

To put limits to our desires and our hopes means that we reject the infinite goodness of God. (C 61)

Jesus does not demand great actions, but only abandonment and gratitude. (C 63)

How sweet is the way of love! We can fall, of course; we can commit many infidelities, but, quoting St. John of the Cross, "love knows how to draw profit from everything and it quickly consumes whatever might have displeased Jesus." (C 65)

I assure you that the good Lord is much kinder than you can imagine. He is satisfied with a glance, with a sigh of love. (C 66)

Does He not notice our anguish and the weight that oppresses us? . . . If He is begging for this sadness we suffer, it must be because He needs it. (C 168)

Everything is not for the worse; everything is for the better. (C 189)

He alone disposes the events of our life of exile. . . . It is the hand of Jesus that guides everything. (C 215)

Is it still possible to have doubts about the designs that Jesus has regarding our souls? (C 215)

Jesus does not need books or doctors to teach souls. He, the Doctor of doctors, teaches without the noise of words. I have never heard Him speak and yet I know He is in me. At every moment, He guides me and inspires me. (C 244)

Love can accomplish all things. Things that are most impossible become easy where love is at work. (C 83)

Remember that nothing is small in the eyes of God. Do all that you do with love. (V 4)

Just as the sun shines equally on the cedar and the little flower, so the Divine Sun shines equally on everyone, great and small. (S 3)

God has given me such a faithful heart that once I love, I love for always. (S 56)

Faith and hope give way to love; we had found already the One we were seeking. (S 70)

In spite of all obstacles, God accomplishes what He wills.

(S 97)

He works miracles even for those whose faith is like a tiny mustard seed, to make it grow. (S 102)

I felt I really was a queen, and I took advantage of my title to get all the favors I could from the King for His ungrateful subjects.... I wanted all the sinners of the world to be converted ... and Purgatory emptied of every single captive. (S 121)

At the bottom of my chalice there was peace, always peace. (S 122)

In little things, as much as big ones, God gives even in this life a hundredfold to those who have left everything for love of Him. (S 131)

The Lord is the rock upon which I stand. (S 148)

By allowing me to endure temptations against faith, the Divine Master has greatly increased in my heart the spirit of faith. (S 151)

My task seems all the more simple; there was only one thing for me to do, unite myself more and more to God, knowing that He would give all the rest in addition. (S 167–68)

Jesus has chosen to show me the only way which leads to the Divine Furnace of love; it is the way of childlike self-surrender, the way of a child who sleeps, afraid of nothing, in its father's arms. (S 192)

God has always helped me, leading me by the hand since my childhood, and I rely upon Him now. Though I should endure the extremity of suffering, I know He will be there with me. (S 212)

How little we know of the goodness and merciful love of Jesus. (C 41)

It is my weakness that gives me confidence. (C 44)

Leave everything in His hands without keeping anything in reserve. (C 57)

I would become discouraged if I did not have faith, or, rather, if I did not love the good Lord. (C 189)

Yes, my God! Yes, my God, I accept anything. (C 191)

I am happy to be able to suffer what Jesus desires me to suffer. If He does not Himself directly prick His little ball, it is true nevertheless that He guides the hands that prick it. (C 201)

There are so few people who do not make their own limited understanding the measure of God's power. (S 142)

We sometimes seem to have been abandoned ... but Jesus ... sees our sorrow and His sweet voice is suddenly heard, a voice sweeter than the rustle of spring.

(C 242)

Nothing is impossible to love. (S 80)

The thought of God's majesty and greatness will put my own small troubles in their place. I will love Him alone and not make myself unhappy by being taken up with trivialities. (S 88)

The thought of Heaven made me supremely happy. It seemed impossible that anyone could be so wicked as to have no faith. They could not possibly be sincere in denying the existence of another world. (S 144)

Oh, what annoying company we are to ourselves when Jesus is not present ... but ... He is not far away. He is right there, quite near and looking at us. Indeed, He is there begging us to offer Him our sorrow. (C 82)

THE SECOND GLORIOUS MYSTERY

THE ASCENSION OF JESUS INTO HEAVEN

Hope

Ask, and it will be given you; seek, and you will find; knock, and it will be opened to you.—Luke 11:9

We never have too much confidence in the good Lord who is so powerful and merciful. We obtain from Him as much as we hope for. (C 20)

In order to remain a little child, we must expect everything from our good Lord, as a child expects everything from his father, without worrying about anything. (C 49)

When I fall on the road I can quickly rise again and Jesus takes me by the hand. (C 42)

It is confidence and confidence alone that should lead us to Love. (C 51)

Justice itself, and justice even more than any other divine perfection, seems to me to be clothed in love. (C 60)

That justice which frightens so many souls is for me a source of joy and confidence. To be just means more than to be severe in punishing the guilty. It takes account of right intentions and wishes to reward virtue.

(C 61)

It is because He is just that He is compassionate and full of mildness, slow to punish and rich in mercy. (C 61)

God knows our weakness. He remembers that we are but dust. As a father is tender towards his children, so is the Lord compassionate towards us. (C 61)

A lack of confidence offends Jesus and wounds His Heart. (C 61)

O Jesus! allow me to declare to You, in my boundless gratitude, that your love is folly! And how could I fail to take my flight to You while I contemplate such a folly, or place a limit on my confidence in You? (C 163)

Abandon [yourself] with absolute confidence to [His] infinite mercy. (C 63)

He measures His gifts according to the amount of confidence He finds in us. (C 64)

The good Lord, who loves us so much, already suffers enough because He sees Himself obliged to leave us on earth to go through our time of trial, and He must be glad when He sees us smile. (C 145)

When we love, we are inclined to say a thousand foolish things. My heaven, then, was nothing but love and in my ardor I felt that there was nothing that could separate me from the divine Object that ravished my heart. (C 231)

He is so beautiful, so ravishing, even when He remains silent, even when He hides Himself.... He is even so much closer when He hides Himself. (C 234)

Jesus does not wish to give me provisions for the future. He feeds me from moment to moment. (C 243)

You would desire to shower it [a soul] with even greater favors, if that soul abandoned itself to Your infinite mercy with entire confidence. (C 245)

God is too good, too generous to give His favors meagerly. (C 271)

A place is kept for us if we but love Him dearly together with our Father and the Spirit of Love. (V 109)

The whole of nature, in fact, enchanted me and raised my soul toward Heaven. (S 15)

Every time my confession gave me a foretaste of eternal happiness. (S 24)

I thought of my heart as a tiny ship with white and graceful sails gliding down the middle of a path of gold, and I resolved that I would never sail it out of the sight of Jesus, so that it might voyage swiftly and in peace toward the shores of Heaven. (S 32)

I hope in Him who is Virtue and Sanctity itself; He alone, content with my frail efforts, will lift me up to Himself, clothe me with His own merits and make me a Saint. (S 48)

God would never inspire me with desires which cannot be realized; so, in spite of my littleness, I can hope to be a Saint. (S 140)

Your arms, My Jesus, are the elevator which will take me up to Heaven. There is no need for me to grow up; on the contrary, I must stay little, and become more and more so. (S 141)

There in the heart of Mother Church I will be love, so shall I be all things, so shall my dreams come true.
(S 199–200)

I have given nothing but love to God and He will repay with love. (S 213)

I expect as much from the justice of our good Lord as from His mercy. (C 61)

He alone can satisfy the multitude of my desires. (S 130)

Because I am so weak, You have been pleased to grant my childish little desires, and now You will grant the rest, other desires far greater than the Universe. (S 198)

I still had an ardent desire for Heaven, though Heaven meant nothing to me, save love, and I was sure that nothing could take me from the Divine Being who held me captive. (S 78)

The Third Glorious Mystery

The Descent of the Holy Spirit

Love of God

> [Y]ou shall love the Lord your God with all your heart, and
> with all your soul, and with all your mind, and with all your
> strength.—Mark 12:30

The proper characteristic of love is that it stoops down
. . . it must stoop down even to nothingness and trans-
form that nothingness into fire. (C 7)

God stoops down to our nothingness and transforms
that nothingness into fire. (C 51)

Jesus will come for us, however far we may be from
Him, and will set us afire with His love. (C 51)

When with childlike confidence we cast our faults into
the devouring furnace of Love, how can they fail to be
consumed forever? (C 65)

I at least wish to tell Him repeatedly that I love Him.
Even if it seemed to me that the fire of love had gone

out, I still would want to cast something in it, and I know for sure that Jesus would revive it. (c 233)

When we love God our heart expands, and we can give incomparably more tender love to those who are dear to us than when our love is selfish and barren. (c 146)

If You should find souls that offer themselves as victims of holocaust to Your merciful love, You would quickly consume them; You would be glad to release the floods of infinite tenderness that are contained in You. (c 150–51)

We are consumed by Love only when we deliver ourselves to Love. (c 158)

O Jesus, I have finally discovered my vocation. My vocation is LOVE ... in the heart of my mother, the Church, it shall be my function to love. In this way I shall be able to be all things, to have all vocations. (c 162)

O Divine Word! You are the Eagle I love, the Eagle who draws me to Himself. Plunging down to this land of exile, You chose to suffer, that You might attract souls to the eternal Furnace of the Blessed Trinity. (c 163)

Eternal Eagle, You desire to nourish me with Your divine substance, who am poor and little and would return to nothingness, were it not that Your divine glance sustains my life at every instant. (c 163)

Obtain for me the favor of flying to the sun of Love, on the wings of the Divine Eagle Himself. (C 163–64)

God is admirable, but He is, above all, lovable. Let us, then, love Him! (C 169–70)

Love will not wear out the fabric of my life; it will rupture it all at once. (C 208–9)

It is impossible to create such sentiments in ourselves. It is the Holy Ghost who imparts them to us. (C 218)

We must keep the fire of our love going. We have no wood when we are in the state of aridity and dark-ness.... He likes to see us feeding it a little. Such a gesture gives Him pleasure. He then throws in much wood. We don't see it but we feel the vehement heat of love. (C 233)

He is not alone; with Him are the two other Persons of the Blessed Trinity who have come to take possession of our soul. (C 242)

An invisible hand had plunged me into a fire; and what a fire, burning, yet full of sweetness! (C 243)

It is by loving You [Jesus] that I draw the Father to me; my poor heart clings to Him and holds Him and will not let Him go. O Trinity, You are the prisoner of my love! (C 264)

I do not want to give in order to receive. I am not a self-seeker. It is God that I love and not myself. (C 79–80)

Your love ... has grown with me and now, it is an abyss of which I cannot sound the depth. Love attracts love. (C 76)

Jesus burns with love for us. (C 266)

I prepared myself with great care for the coming of the Holy Spirit; I can't understand how anyone could do otherwise before receiving this Sacrament of Love.
(S 54–55)

How happy I was! Like the Apostles, I waited for the promised Holy Spirit and was overjoyed that soon I would be a perfect Christian and have my forehead sealed eternally with the mystic cross of this great Sacrament. (S 55)

Jesus, the Eternal Fire ... burns without consuming.
(S 56)

Purgatory holds no fears for me. . . . The Fire of Love is far more sanctifying than the fires there. (S 137)

All the friends of God have followed the guidance of the Holy Spirit. (S 140)

I want Jesus so to draw me into the flames of His love, so to make me one with Himself that He may live and act in me. I feel that the more the fire of love inflames my heart, the more I shall say, "Draw me." (S 188)

Souls on fire with love cannot remain inactive. (S 189)

Be disposed to receive the benefits of His consuming and transforming love working within us. (C 50)

I count only on love. Ask the good Lord that all the prayers that are said for me may serve to increase the fire that must consume me. (C 209)

He puts Himself at our mercy. He does not want to accept anything from us unless we give it with a good heart. He stretches out His hand to us to receive a little love. (C 235)

When my youthful heart was afire with the flame we call love, You came and claimed it for Yourself. (C 75)

What I seek is love. I want nothing else but to love you, O Jesus. (C 80)

Little things done out of love are those that charm the Heart of Christ. . . . The most brilliant deeds, when done without love, are but nothingness. (C 139)

THE FOURTH GLORIOUS MYSTERY

THE ASSUMPTION OF MARY
INTO HEAVEN

Desire for Heaven

*Come, O blessed of my Father, inherit the kingdom prepared
for you from the foundation of the world.*—Matthew 25:34

I will spend my heaven in doing good upon earth. Why
not, since the Angels can take care of us while still en-
joying the Beatific Vision? (S 213)

If my wishes are granted, my heaven will be spent on
earth until the end of the world. (C 21)

When the Angel shall have said "time is no more" then
will I rest. I shall then be able to rejoice because the
number of the elect will be complete and all shall have
entered into joy and repose. (C 21)

I feel always the same audacious confidence that I will
become a great saint, for I do not count on my own
merits since I have none, but I hope in Him. (C 53)

It is He and He alone who, being satisfied with my feeble efforts, will raise me to Himself and, covering me with His infinite merits, will make me a saint. (C 53–54)

If we abandon ourselves, and place our confidence in God, while making every small effort and hoping everything from His mercy, we shall be rewarded as much as the greatest saints. (C 53)

Jesus does not take time into consideration, for time does not exist in heaven. He has merely to consider love. (C 68)

One glance, one moment of His Heart can cause His flower to open out for all eternity. (C 68)

I trust, O my adorable Eagle, that some day, You will come and take Your little bird and, mounting with him to the Furnace of Love, You will plunge him for all eternity in the flaming abyss of that Love. (C 164)

If it is necessary to suffer and weep in order to reach heaven, well, I want to suffer whatever may please Jesus.
(C 170)

If Jesus, in spite of His love for us, makes us suffer, if He does not spare us, it is because He looks beyond time, because He already beholds us in the state of glory. (C 170)

Life passes so quickly. How much better to have a beautiful crown at the expense of a little pain than to have an ordinary one without pain. (C 171)

Think of it, for one pain borne with joy, I shall love God more perfectly for all eternity! (C 171)

Let us embrace suffering, otherwise Jesus will not be able to say "now it is my turn to give you something."

(C 171)

I reflect . . . I think about the good Lord; I think of how quickly this life is passing; I think of eternity. (C 228)

I don't see very well what more I shall possess in heaven than here on earth. Of course in heaven I shall see the good Lord, but when it comes to being with Him, I already have this entirely. (C 250)

When they have entered their heavenly country, they may love one another, with a grateful love, a love much greater than any that could ever be found among the members of the most ideal family of earth. (C 270)

Eternal reward has no proportion to our small sacrifices in this life. (C 80)

The most holy souls are perfect only in heaven. (C 72)

Life passes. Eternity comes to meet us with great strides. Soon, we shall be living with the very life of Jesus . . .

we shall be deified in the very source of all joys, of all delights. (V 125)

[I] longed for Heaven, my true home, where it would be always Sunday. (S 26)

Darkness falls even on the brightest day. Only the first day of Communion in eternity will never end. (S 53)

I seem to look into infinity, to reach the eternal shore where Jesus embraces me. I can see Mary coming to meet me. . . . I already seem to enjoy that family life which lasts for all eternity. (S 62)

What will an eternal Communion be like in the House of the King of Heaven? . . . His house will be all our own forever and ever. (S 91)

It is His palace of glory that He is keeping for us, and we shall see Him then, not in the guise of a child or under the form of bread, but as He is, radiant in His infinite beauty. (S 91)

The very desires and intuitions of my inmost heart assured me that another and more lovely land awaited me, an abiding city—just as the genius of Christopher Columbus gave him a presentiment of a new world. (S 145–46)

I sing of Heaven's happiness, of what it is to possess God forever. (S 147)

I will follow You throughout the boundless spaces of eternity, singing Your new Canticle, the Canticle of LOVE. (S 161)

O Jesus, if the desire of love brings such delight, what must it be really to possess it and enjoy it for eternity! (S 203)

It is only that which is eternal that is capable of satisfying our heart. (C 112)

The Fifth Glorious Mystery

The Crowning of Mary Queen of Heaven and Earth

❧

Devotion to Mary

Behold, your mother!
—John 19:27

Not being able to bear it any longer, I asked the Blessed Virgin to take my head in her hands and to support it.

(C 189)

The Blessed Virgin is my mother and little children ordinarily resemble their mama. (C 275)

How great the fervor with which I begged her to be always my protector and to help me realize my dream, hiding me in the shadow of her virginal mantle! (C 276)

How much I should have liked to be a priest so that I might have preached about the Virgin Mary. (C 277)

The Blessed Virgin is the Queen of heaven and earth, quite true, but she is more mother than queen. (C 277)

It is proper to speak of her prerogatives, but we must not content ourselves with that. We must do all we can to make her beloved of souls. (C 277)

[The Blessed Virgin] loves us truly as Jesus loves us. (C 278)

I felt that the Blessed Virgin was watching over me, that I was her child. Hence I found it necessary to call her "Mama", for this name seemed even more tender than that of mother. (C 279)

When we ask a grace from the Blessed Virgin, we receive immediate help. Have you not experienced this? Well, try it and you will see. (C 279)

The Blessed Virgin never fails to protect me as soon as I invoke her. In my troubles and anxieties I very quickly turn towards her and, like the most tender of mothers, she always takes care of my interests. (C 279)

To ask something of the Blessed Virgin is not the same thing as asking it of the good Lord. She knows very well what to do with my little wishes, whether to transmit them [to God] or not. . . . If, after that, we obtain nothing, it is because what we asked for is not in accordance with God's designs. (C 279)

When we have prayed to the Blessed Virgin and she has not given us what we asked for, we should let her do what she pleases, without insisting on our request; and after that let us not worry any more about it. (C 279)

I like to hide my pains from the good Lord, because I want to give Him the impression that I am always happy; but I hide nothing from the Blessed Virgin; to her I tell everything. (C 280)

The Blessed Virgin will never be hidden from me, for I love her too much. (C 281)

During this sorrowful exile, O my beloved Mother, I want to live with you, and then follow you to heaven some day. (C 282)

My good Holy Virgin, I see that I am happier than you, for I have you for a mother, but you have no blessed virgin whom you can love. (C 282)

O Mary, if I were Queen of Heaven and you were Thérèse, I would rather become Thérèse, that you might be the Queen of Heaven. (C 282)

You came to smile at me in the morning of my life; come and smile at me again, . . . Mother, now that it is eventide. (C 283)

She has given us so many proofs that she cares for us like a Mother. (V 142)

A mother's heart always understands, even when her child can do no more than lisp. (S 4)

I can't describe what I experienced at her Shrine. The graces she gave me there were like those of my First Communion, filling me with peace and happiness. (S 86)

She [our Lady] already occupied a very large place in my heart, but I promised to give her even more. (S 24)

The Queen of Heaven was keeping faithful watch over her little flower, smiling down on her from above. She was ready to calm the storm. (S 39)

The insight of the most skilled doctors can't compare with that of a mother's heart. (S 40)

There was a sun not far away to which the petals of the "little flower" would often turn—the statue of the Queen of Heaven. (S 42)

I made up my mind that I must consecrate myself in some special way to Our Lady. (S 61)

The sufferings of Jesus pierced the heart of His Mother, so the sufferings and humiliations of the ones we love the best on earth pierce ours. (S 114)

Our Lady was helping me to prepare a wedding garment for my soul. (S 118)

I think of my soul as a piece of waste ground and ask Our Lady to take away the rubbish of my imperfections and then build a spacious tabernacle there, worthy of Heaven, adorning it with her own loveliness. (S 129)

I will never cease to bless the Mother who gave [me] to Jesus. [I] will eternally rejoice to be a flower in her crown; with her [I] will eternally sing the canticle of love and gratitude that is ever new. (S 137)

I take refuge in prayer; I have only to turn to Mary, and Jesus triumphs over everything. (S 171)

I felt entirely hidden under the veil of the Blessed Mother. (C 242)

The Blessed Virgin is sometimes pictured as if she were unapproachable. We should realize on the contrary that it is possible to imitate her by practicing her hidden virtues. (C 277)

Mary my Mother made it quite clear to me that it was really she who had smiled on me and cured me. With all my heart I begged her to keep me far from all occasions of sin and to make my dream come true of casting about me her mantle of virginity. (S 86)

OTHER TOPICS

Prayer

Watch and pray that you may not enter into temptation.
—Mark 14:38

I am suffering too much; so I am praying. (C 190)

As for myself, prayer is a lifting up of the heart. It is a simple glance towards heaven, a cry of gratitude and love in the midst of trials as well as joys. (C 259)

It [prayer] is something great, something supernatural, which dilates the soul and unites it to Jesus. (C 259)

I greatly love prayers said in common, for Jesus has promised to be in the midst of those who are assembled in His Name. (C 270)

It is God's will that those who are still in this world should communicate heavenly gifts to one another by means of prayers. (C 270)

Perhaps all the graces that I have received in abundance have come through the prayers of some little soul whom I shall know only in heaven! (C 271)

Is not the apostolate of prayer, as it were, more sublime than the work of actually preaching? (C 105)

When I am incapable of praying, I want to keep telling Him that I love Him. It's not difficult, and it keeps the fire going. (V 43)

Prayer was my one consolation. (S 75)

We must set to work and pray very hard. (S 172)

The power of prayer is certainly wonderful. One might liken it to a queen who always has free access to the king and can obtain everything she asks. (S 172)

I just act like a child who can't read; I tell God, quite simply, all that I want to say, and He always understands. (C 173)

Whenever my soul is so dry that I am incapable of a single good thought, I always say an "Our Father" or a "Hail Mary" very slowly, and these prayers alone cheer me up and nourish my soul with divine food. (S 173)

All my strength lies in prayer and sacrifice. They are my invincible arms, and I know from experience that I can conquer hearts with these more surely than I can with words. (S 171)

I take refuge in prayer; I have only to turn to Mary, and Jesus triumphs over everything. (S 171)

I have many distractions, but as soon as I am aware of them, I pray for those people the thought of whom is diverting my attention. In this way, they reap the benefit of my distractions. (V 43)

[Mental prayer is] ... the furnace which should inflame everything with the fire of love. (C 257)

The Eucharist

❦

He who eats my flesh and drinks my blood has eternal life,
and I will raise him up at the last day.—John 6:54

Although You have re-ascended to Light inaccessible, Your permanent abode, You deign to remain in this valley of tears, hidden under the appearances of a white Host. (C 163)

I don't think it is too much to suffer, for the sake of gaining one Communion. (C 195)

[After Communion] It is now no longer I who live; but Christ lives in me. (C 226)

The very day after my Communion ... I was flooded with such extraordinary consolation that I look upon it as one of the greatest graces in my life. (C 226)

Our Lord does not come down from Heaven every day to lie in a golden ciborium. He comes to find another heaven which is infinitely dearer to Him—the heaven of our souls, created in His Image, the living temples of the Adorable Trinity. (V 85)

Do you realize that Jesus is there in the tabernacle expressly for you, for you alone? He burns with the desire to come into your heart. (V 85)

Kneeling before the tabernacle, I can think of only one thing to say to our Lord: "My God, you know that I love you." And I feel that my prayer does not weary Jesus; knowing my weakness, He is satisfied with my good will. (V 96)

On that day [First Communion] it was more than a meeting—it was a complete fusion. We were no longer two, for Thérèse had disappeared like a drop of water lost in the mighty ocean. Jesus alone remained—the Master and the King. (S 52)

All Heaven entered my soul when I received Jesus, . . . it was joy alone, deep ineffable joy that filled my heart. (S 52)

I longed for nothing but to receive Him. (S 54)

I had the indescribable happiness of going to Communion every day. How wonderful it was . . . what a supreme joy to be united to my Beloved every day! (S 128)

If only I were a priest! How lovingly I would bear You in my hands, my Jesus, when my voice had brought You down from Heaven. (S 197)

The procession of the Blessed Sacrament was what I loved best, for I could scatter flowers beneath the feet of God! (S 25)

I wanted to give Him consolation, to draw near to the tabernacle, to be watched over, tended and gathered by Him. (S 47)

Here, in the silence, I found my one consolation: Jesus, my only friend. (S 61)

THE CHURCH

So now I say to you: You are Peter and on this rock I will build my Church. And the gates of the underworld can never hold out against it.—Matthew 16:18

What a beautiful vocation is ours, to preserve the salt by which souls are preserved. (C 8)

Feast days! Those words conjure up more wonderful memories! I did so love them ... that again was a foretaste of Heaven. (S 24–25)

Missionaries are best helped by prayer and sacrifice. (S 183)

I want to be "a daughter of the Church" and pray for all the intentions of the Vicar of Christ. This is my one great aim. (S 184)

I long to bring light to souls, like the prophets and doctors; to go to the ends of the earth to preach Your name, to plant Your glorious Cross, my Beloved, on pagan shores. (S 197)

One mission field alone would never be enough; all the world, even its remotest islands, must be my mission field. (S 197)

As I thought about the Church's Mystical Body, I could not see myself in any of the members mentioned by St. Paul, or rather, I wanted to see myself in all of them. (S 199)

I saw that the Church must have a heart, that this heart must be on fire with love. (S 199)

I am a child of Holy Church, and the Church is a Queen, because she is espoused to You, the King of Kings. (S 201)

I love You, Jesus! I love Mother Church, and I never forget that the least act of pure love is of more value to her than all other works put together. (S 203)

All is well when one seeks nothing but the Divine Will; that is why the little flower obeys Jesus by trying to please those who hold His place on earth. (S 140)

There is no heroic deed I do not wish to perform. I feel as daring as a crusader, ready to die for the Church upon the battlefield. (S 197)

I offer every step for some missionary who, far away, is exhausted by his work for souls; I offer my exhaustion to relieve his. (S 208)

THE BIBLE

Heaven and earth will pass away, but my words will not pass away.—Matthew 24:6

I had not yet discovered the hidden treasures of the Gospels. (S 69)

I am rescued from this helpless state by the Scriptures and "The Imitation", finding in them a hidden manna, pure and substantial. (S 135)

During meditation I am sustained above all else by the Gospels. They supply my poor soul's every need. (S 135)

They [the Gospels] are always yielding up to me new lights and mysterious hidden meanings. (S 135)

Draw upon the riches opened up by Our Lord in the Gospels. I search the depths of His adorable words.

(S 161)

The Saints

The virtuous will shine like the sun in the kingdom of their Father.—Matthew 13:43

When we grieve because of our incapacity to do good, our only resource is to offer the works of others. Herein lies the advantage of the Communion of Saints. (C 270)

Peace soon filled my soul, and I knew that I was loved, not only by those on earth, but by those in Heaven too. (S 63)

I not only believed that Heaven existed, I knew it; and I knew too that it was full of souls who loved me as their own child. (S 196)

I know that all the eagles in Your heavenly court look compassionately down on me, protecting me and defending me, putting to flight the demon vultures who seek to prey on me. (S 205)

I turn to God and the Saints. . . . I thank them, for I am sure they only want to see how far I am going to trust them. (S 211)

My foolishness lies in hoping that Your love accepts me ... it lies in counting on the Angels and Saints to help me. (S 205)